HOW TO IMPROVE THE PERFORMANCE OF YOUR COMPANY

MANAGING PEOPLE TO GET BETTER RESULTS

by Martin Prodaj

For more visit my web page www.martinprodaj.com

Copyright

Disclaimer

The information contained in this book and is meant to serve as a comprehensive collection of ideas and tips. Summaries, strategies, tips and tricks are only recommendations by the author, and reading this eBook does not guarantee that one's results will exactly mirror our own results. The author of this book made all reasonable efforts to provide current and accurate information for the readers of this eBook. The authors will not be held liable for any unintentional errors or omissions that may be found.

The material in this book may include information, products, or services by third parties. As such, the author of this guide does not assume responsibility or liability for any Third Party Material or opinions.

The publication of such Third Party materials does not constitute the authors' guarantee of any information, instruction, opinion, products or service contained within the Third Party Material. Use of recommended Third Party Material does not guarantee that your results will mirror our own. Publication of such Third Party Material is simply a recommendation and expression of the authors' own opinion of that material.

Free Gift

As a way of saying thank you for buying my book, I want to invite you to grab a free check list for creating a perfect workshop in your company. You can grab it here.

TABLE OF CONTENTS

INTRODUCTION

Education, if analysed beyond its traditional limits, is at the core of all our actions. Everything that we do is based on what we have learnt, whether through instruction, vision or adaptation. Our minds are constantly analysing and processing new data, and we have the potential to learn much more than we think. On the other hand, we are the ones who prevent ourselves from broadening our horizons by placing constraints on ourselves. Education can also be viewed in a corporate context. Most companies would rather hire an educated candidate than one who isn't, because they know that that particular candidate will not require much on-the-job training. In most cases, the company will then stop investing in the education of that employee. Although companies like to talk about investing in their employees, they rarely give it the seriousness it deserves. It should not be forgotten that it is people who determine the competitiveness and capabilities of a company. The employees need to constantly learn new things and systems in order to improve efficiency in the workplace. Investing in corporate education is indeed a worthy endeavour. In this book, we will try to show you how corporate education can be utilised and the factors to take into account while doing so. I hope that this book will prove helpful in the subject, and in case you encounter an issue you are not familiar with, or you would like some assistance with corporate and technical training, I would be pleased to work with you.

CHAPTER 1
SELECTING THE RIGHT PERSON
FOR THE JOB

Choosing the right candidate to employ for your organisation is not an easy task. I know firsthand how difficult it is to take that first step of selecting an employee who is suited to the company. It requires vision, foresight, and the uncanny ability to read the candidates mind. The questions that the interviewer asks the candidate have to be the right ones; questions that will help determine if the candidate can handle what is required of him or her. This is a process that cannot be rushed, and most companies need to realise that you cannot assume a candidate will fit the company. You have to get it right the first time. Choosing the right candidate is both a decision making and cognitive process, but when done the right way, it is the company that will benefit.

THE SELECTION PROCESS

The selection process is one that requires an investment in time, money and preparation. It is therefore important that you decide how you want to go about it. There are two options here: You can outsource the short listing process or you can conduct the interviews yourself. Each of these options has its pros and cons. Outsourcing the candidate selection process to an agency saves you time, but will cost more. If you choose to conduct the selection process yourself, then be prepared to save money but spend a lot of time and energy.

The person entrusted with the task of selecting the right candidate must understand one basic and crucial principle: If you want to get the right person for the job, you have to know exactly what kind of candidate you want. You should start by preparing a basic personal or working profile of the candidate. You should ask yourself what kind of qualities you want to see in the candidate, and then develop a way of finding those qualities by interacting with the candidate.

The questions that you ask the candidate during the interview process should be specific to the role they are to play in the company. I know that most interviewers tend to generalise their questions, and this will definitely not help you to get the best person for the job. Forming an opinion based on general views will not help your company to scout for the best talent out there.

You should also take into consideration the kind of position you intend to fill. The strategies that you employ when filling a managerial position are quite different from those used when looking for ordinary employees. You should be able to factor this in when choosing the right candidate for a job.

There are certain aspects of a candidate that you should focus on if you are to pick the best of the bunch. These are:

- Look for a candidate who is a consistent performer i.e. a results-oriented person. Remember, this employee you are hiring is going to be earning a salary, and you need to make sure they work for it. You should be able to determine this by asking relevant questions that will get them to explain their past work results. You should always structure your questions in a systematic manner. Random questions will not help you to determine whether the candidate is a performer or has poor work ethics. You should go through the candidate's resume to design your line of questioning.
- You should look at their achievements and what they have done in the past by looking at their resume. A resume will give you an indication of the candidates past and how they performed in their previous jobs. The

resume is a true picture of the achievements the candidate has had professionally. You should also look at their references and do background checks.

- Understand the objectives of the candidate. What does the candidate expect from the job? What are their intentions? You should ask the candidate these questions so that you understand their goals for getting the job. I know of candidates who applied for jobs simply because they wanted to get away from their old boss; some just want a salary increment; others do it for the adventure of a new challenge. You should be keen on the kind of questions the candidate asks, as these are what you use to determine their priorities. If they want the job simply for the money, then their questions will focus mostly on the salary.

- Take into account the corporate culture of the organisation. Every company has its own unique culture – for example some are formal, others are informal. You should consider whether the candidate will fit into the company and if not, what you can do to help them do so. You do not want to hire someone who will not fundamentally fit in with the other employees, as this means they might run away after a short time. The modern work place is not what it used to be, where an employee stayed with one company for decades. Times have changed and so have working practices.

At the end of it all, you need to make a decision, one that is based on concrete judgement and solid reasoning. Picking the best talent from the market is an integral part of every company out there. The right candidate will never pop out of nowhere or fall on your lap. You have to put in the time, money and effort to find them – like a needle in a haystack. Now that the first step is over and you have got your perfect candidate, the job is half way done. The next thing you have to worry about is how you are going to keep the candidate in the company.

CHAPTER 2
DEVELOPING THE RIGHT
CORPORATE CULTURE

Corporate culture can be referred to as the values, beliefs, behaviours, attitudes and philosophies that members of an organisation share. A company's corporate culture is what determines the interaction between employees, management, and the outside world, and ultimately defines its nature.

Importance of Corporate Culture

The culture that a company adopts is what makes it what it is. The corporate culture of one company can be quite different from another, and such a distinction can be the difference between having good, highly motivated employees and having unmotivated workers. It is actually similar to an ethnic culture except it contains people from various backgrounds. Such a diverse cultural connection can lead to creativity and understanding that will enhance the work environment and produce better results.

The importance of a good corporate culture is what will separate you from the rest of your competitors as it creates a unique company brand that your employees will want to associate with. It also serves the purpose of defining your company's set procedures and standards that guide the company and its employees in the right direction. A good corporate culture should be one that brings all your employees together, allows them to learn from one another, and encourages them to do their best for the benefit of them and the company.

Types of corporate culture

1. Traditional.

This can be described as an old-fashioned approach to the work environment. A traditional corporate culture tends to have clear and distinct roles for every employee. There is usually very little room for deviation from orders given, and disagreement is not allowed. The chain of command is clear in such organisations, with work procedures and standards being enforced strictly. Although such a culture may seem unreasonable to some, it does have its uses. A traditional culture can be the most effective way of running a company that is already well-established and incorporates tried-and-tested methods of doing business.

2. Innovative

This type of corporate culture is the opposite of the traditional one. An innovative culture actually encourages its employees to be creative, take their own initiative, and even tweak the standard procedures when necessary. The principle behind this is that by allowing the employees room to experiment and take risks, they will come up with creative ideas that will propel the business forward. The danger with having such a work environment is that it is risky; some ideas will fail inevitably and the lack of proper, laid down procedures will result in wastage of time and resources. Companies that adopt this kind of corporate culture should always consider whether or not the creative breakthroughs justify the risks.

3. Highly skilled (Baseball team)

This does not mean that the other types of cultures do not have highly skilled workers or teams. What it refers to is the emphasis that certain companies place on recruiting the best – and only the best – talent there is in the market place. Such a company will only be interested in hiring people who can get the job done and boost the organisations bottom line. A highly skilled corporate culture is usually found in firms that engage in high risk operations, such as financial speculation. These companies are constantly trying to stay ahead of the competition, and they therefore have to attract the best and brightest in the field to do this. The problem with this kind of culture is that there is a high staff turnover rate as employees are constantly being poached by rivals.

4. <u>Social</u>

What defines a social corporate culture is the premium it put in developing teamwork, joint efforts, and employee relationships built on trust. It usually puts a lot of emphasis on making sure that the workers are taken care of. The driving philosophy behind such a work environment is simple - it's important to pay workers slightly higher wages than normal, to identify and reward achievements, and motivate everyone to participate. The company wants to take the time to develop and foster employees who are loyal and skilled, instead of kicking out someone who seems unqualified. These types of organisations are usually bound by a sense of pride and identity that employees derive from their work.

<u>Five Signs of a Company with Good Corporate Culture</u>

All companies crave a work environment where the employees and management share the same objectives, feel included, and participate in making the organisation better. It is very important for an organisation to pay attention to the signs of its corporate culture, as this will help it to stay on course and achieve its mission.

1. There is emphasis on purpose

A good company must develop a clear and definite purpose and establish the attitude that purpose is more vital to success than process. The supervisors within the company should actually be looking out for effectiveness and efficiency of employees instead of focusing on whether the proper procedures were followed to the letter. With an emphasis on purpose, sometimes there will be a shift from merely churning out large quantities of products to focusing on the quality of the output. It no longer about the number of pages the employee's report contains or the number of calls they made – it is about the efficiency of the report and the success of the calls made.

2. The employees are fulfilled

Any company with a good culture will naturally find itself with employees who are happy and fulfilled, and are working without fear. What most companies need to understand is that having employees who are satisfied in their work environment leads to improved competitiveness, productivity, and performance. Satisfied employees are simply more willing to stay at work till late, go the extra mile, and come up with new solutions without being asked.

3. The company has an effective style of management

We are all well aware of the different styles of management that exist in different companies. What you need to know is that some work, while others do not. In order to manage your staff effectively and achieve better results, you need to have effective leaders and managers who are more focused on creating a team that can come together, pool their individual skills, and come up with innovative strategies. A company that has a dictatorial manager who misuses power over the subordinates simply for the sake of it will weaken the system. It is important to have the company supervisors play more of a coaching role by letting the employees work independently but availing themselves in case any difficulties come up.

4. The company is adaptable

Change is inevitable in life - there is no way around the fact. An organisation that has a good corporate culture usually wants to stay competitive in the market, and this requires it to adapt to the changing environment. Opportunities must be seized when they arise, and unexpected problems must be solved when they come up. Organisations that place more value on precedence than flexibility tend to have work cultures that are restrictive and the employees will not bother to be creative or efficient.

5. The company is realistic

A sign of a good company is that it is realistic. This means that difficult times should be faced with solutions that are realistic instead of trying to hide the fact from your employees. There should be more focus on reality, instead of form.

Shaping Your Corporate Culture through Education and Training

Education and training of employees plays a special role within a company. It is important that your company develops a culture that promotes the participation of its staff in training courses that will help them learn new systems and strategies for improving efficiency in the workplace. A really effective training program should be designed to have a sustainable, measurable, and meaningful impact on corporate culture. Shaping your corporate culture is a long-term endeavour that requires the coordination of the efforts of all company departments. It should encompass everyone; from the Board, CEO, management, employees, as well as your customers.

The education and training of your employees will significantly improve job performance by maintaining a work environment of trust and diligence. The three key features of an effective training program are:

Purposefulness

The training program has to be developed in a way that ensures the objectives are achieved. The goals have to be clear, and both short and long-term goals and company values have to be developed as part of the initiative.

Pervasiveness

The best and most effective training programs incorporate value messages and emphasise the need for decision making that is based on values that the company holds dear.

Consistency

The training that the employees receive must be consistent, understandable and practical.

The impact of the training on the company will be felt once the messages imparted on the employees become part of the culture. Consequently, there will be rapid change, followed by a positive, measurable and sustained impact.

CHAPTER 3
OBJECTIVES OF EMPLOYEE TRAINING

Every company wants to be successful – that is a fact. The secret lies in figuring out the best way to go about it. The success of a company is built on its workforce. The level of education, training, skills, and knowledge of your employees will have a direct impact on how efficient your business is and how effective it is run. Therefore, it is important for managers to constantly look out for signs of underperformance or lack of motivation in their employees, so that they can take the appropriate measures.

If you have a company that has achieved some measure of success in the past, but has recently experienced reduced levels of growth or efficiency, then you might have to think about training your staff. This also applies to companies that want to boost employees' skills in order to reach a target state. Before you make any decisions regarding the training of employees, there are certain questions that you must ask.

- What are the objectives of this training?

- Which is the best course to implement?

- What exactly is the content of the training course?

- Is the content relevant to our company's objectives?

- Do we even need to train the employees?

- What are the evaluation criteria that will be used to judge the effectiveness of the training?

- Should we conduct the training internally or outsource the process to an agency?

These are serious things that need to be considered before making any major decisions. The main thing is to know what you want to achieve by training your employees. This will make the process much easier for everyone.

The overall goal of an employee training program is to plug the gap between existing and required skills, knowledge and aptitude. It is important at this stage to involve the upper levels of management so as to incorporate the company's objectives into those of the training course.

Some of the objectives of this training could be:

- To ensure that new employees have basic knowledge necessary for proper task performance.

- To expose the employees to the latest trends, strategies and systems in their fields. This will ensure that the company stays up-to-date and relevant with the market needs.

- To widen the outlook of the supervisors, some of who may have narrow views due to many years of specialisation. The training will broaden their minds and give them a chance to exchange experiences with others.

- To train employees in management skills that they may use when the situation arises. This prepares them for upward career mobility in the future.

- To ensure that employees are flexible and prepared for redeployment to other work environments.

- To motivate and provide job satisfaction to employees. Training provides an opportunity to use skills and knowledge that will ultimately enhance company productivity.

- To enhance the individual competency of each employee by providing access to better sources of knowledge and skills.

It is crucial to clearly define the objectives, especially to the employees, so that the training course achieves its targets and by extension, so does the company.

CHAPTER 4
THE APPROPRIATE HR TOOLS FOR EMPLOYEE TRAINING AND DEVELOPMENT

Once you have clearly established what the aims and objectives of employee education are, you should decide which tools or instruments will suit the company best. There are two general forms of training that can be used by a company: on-the-job training and off-the-job training. I have explained below what each of these types entails and the methods involved in each.

On-The-Job Training

This is training that is given to employees of a company while they continue to perform their normal tasks. This method ensures that no time is lost while the training is going on. The employees should be provided with the details as soon as a plan has been developed for the content to be taught. There should also be an established schedule that has regular assessments that tracks the progress of employees. The advantages of this method include instant feedback on performance and quick remedial action if the performance is not up to standard. The disadvantages include possible disruption of work flow and slowing the trainer's production.

On-the-job training techniques include orientations, apprenticeships, job instruction training, coaching, job rotation, and internships.

Orientations

These are specifically designed for new employees. A new employee's first few days are crucial in determining their success in the company. The topics that are usually focused on are

- The background and mission of the company

- The organisation's key members

- The key members in every department, and the importance of each department in achieving the company's mission.

- Employee rules and regulations

Training employees through orientations can be done by using verbal or written presentations. The important thing is for the new employee to understand their new work environment.

Apprenticeships

This kind of training usually involves en employee working with, and for, a skilled senior worker for a long period of time. It is meant to develop employees who can perform many different duties, and allows them to practice a specific trade. This training method is useful for jobs that need production skills.

Job rotations

This involves the movement of an employee through a string of jobs to make sure that they understand the duties that are related to different jobs. This is commonly used in supervisory positions, where the employee will be trained on a little bit of everything. It is useful in companies where one employee can be asked to perform many different jobs.

Internships

This can be described as a combination of on-the-job and classroom training. They are commonly used to educate marketing employees and prospective managers.

Coaching

This is one of the most effective ways to train an employee during their professional development. It must be said, however, that not all problems can be solved through coaching, and not every employee is a good candidate for this training method. The major benefit of coaching is that it directly targets the employee's weak spots, and can be very effective if the employee brings the problem up themselves.

If you would like to learn more about how to coach your employees, you can visit the blog www.koucingblog.org for a 6-part video on the basics of coaching, or go to www.zakladykoucingu.sk for a more comprehensive video course on the "Fundamentals of coaching."

A good coaching program is where the employees volunteer and are willing to develop themselves. They have to be self-motivated because you cannot force someone to accept to be coached against their will. The basic diagnostic feature of a coaching program is that almost no recommendations are made or advice given. You can recognise a good coach by the fact that he or she does not impose solutions on the trainee.

Off-The-Job Training

This includes short courses, workshops, brainstorming, mentoring, role playing/simulation, and e-learning.

Short courses

This is a classic method of educating people, resembling a typical school set up. The advantage with this training technique is that you can educate a large number of people in a relatively short time span. However, it can also serve as a drawback due to the lack of one-on-one interaction with individuals in a large group, and the low memorisation rate. The trainees also tend to find the course boring, but a smart lecturer should be able to make the content interesting. The lecturer might also find it difficult to cover the course in-depth.

Workshops

Workshops require active participation; more than short courses. Workshops can be used when you want to get some feedback from employees, generate ideas, or just share work experiences. This training technique requires a skilled moderator or facilitator and a clear objective of what is to be achieved. It is also necessary to develop a clear structure to avoid people becoming inattentive.

Brainstorming

Everyone has heard of this classic technique. It has one basic principle: Create a space where everyone is allowed to freely contribute their ideas without any form of criticism. The analysis of ideas generated is only done in the second stage, where the ones with greatest potential are selected for implementation.

Mentoring

This is a professional development tool that is used on individual employees, not groups. Unlike coaching, mentoring actually allows ideas and advice on solution of problems to be given to the employee. The mentor is actually expected to advise the employee on what steps to take. The employee is provided with an experienced senior employee, who had previously occupied a similar position, to supervise his or her learning experience. Although the mentor instructs and advises, they do not participate in the performance of the job. The employee gains firsthand experience and consults the mentor whenever they need assistance.

Role-playing/simulation

These training techniques try to create realistic decision making conditions for the employees. Under the simulated situation, there is presentation of probable problems and discussion of alternative solutions. Experienced employees can describe real life experiences to the trainees, and even help them come up with likely solutions. This technique is inexpensive and is often used on management and marketing trainees.

E-learning

This is a modern training solution to education that is becoming more and more prevalent as time goes by. There are numerous advantages to this technique. The first is that the teacher does not sleep, lose their voice or get sick, so services can be accessed 24/7. Once you have purchased the services, you can use them at your own pace. Although this technique has high initial costs of investment, the benefits will eventually surpass the costs if e-learning is used effectively. Inexpensive solutions are available and for only a few hundred Euros, you can own a system that only needs to be filled with content. Such a system can be found at www.mojwebinar.sk. The only thing you need to is to fill the system with content, which you can get from your own company resources, or purchase at www.mojwebinar.sk.

CHAPTER 5
ACCURATE EVALUATION OF THE TRAINING PROGRAMS

The next phase of employee training and development is the evaluation phase. However, evaluation should ideally have begun during the previous stage – implementation – because what you are evaluating are the employees themselves during the training, as well as the training program itself. It is all about getting progressive feedback from everybody involved (supervisors, trainees) in order to improve the training process and ensure that the trainees are achieving the objectives of the training.

The Evaluation Perspectives

There are 4 different levels to look at the evaluation phase. I want you to note that the farther down the list you move, the more compelling the evaluation.

1. Reaction: The feelings of the employee about the training.

2. Learning: The knowledge, facts, e.t.c., gained by the employee.

3. Behaviour: The skills that the employee has developed and how they are using them on the job.

4. Effectiveness or results: Did the employee use the skills they learned to perform their necessary duties, and if so, what were the results achieved?

It is true that level 4 (evaluating the effectiveness and results) is the most desired result of training. However, it is the hardest to accomplish because it requires you to use key measures of performance – tangible measures e.g. quicker and reliable output after a machine operator has completed training, employees reporting higher job satisfaction (via questionnaires) after their supervisor has undergone training, e.t.c. During this period, solid principles of performance management are required.

Considerations for Evaluation the Training

In most cases, the people doing the evaluation look for reliability, accuracy, and validity in their evaluations. This may require more resources (money, time, and people) than the company has. The evaluators also look for relevant and applicable approaches to the evaluation. I have outlined below some basic suggestions that you can consider after the training has been completed.

- Give the employee a test prior to and subsequent to the training and development – then compare the results.

- Conduct an interview of the employee before and after the training, and compare the results.

- Observe the employee as they perform their tasks.

- Invite an expert evaluator – internal or external – to assess the skills and knowledge of the employee.

Post-Training Data collection

Data collection is crucial in the evaluation process. The evaluators should collect both soft data (attitudes, work environment, and work habits) as well as hard data (time, cost, quality, and output). Level 4 data (from the evaluation perspectives described above) can be collected using the methods below:

Follow-up Questionnaires – These can be used to reveal particular applications of training. You can either use forced response questions or open-ended questions. The questionnaires can be used to capture data for both Level 3 and Level 4.

Program Assignments – This method is useful for simple, short-term tasks. The employees are asked to complete the assignment on the job, by applying the knowledge and skills they have learned from the training and development program. The completed assignments are used as evaluation information, containing both Level 3 and Level 4 data. Level 4 data can be converted into monetary values, making it possible to compare the cost of the training to the output i.e. develop the Return on Investment.

Action Plans – These are developed during the training and development program itself, and are to be implemented after completion of the training program. The evaluation information is collected from the follow-up of the plans. Action plans can be useful in collecting Level 3/4 data.

Performance Contracts – These are created before the training is conducted, in agreement with the employee, their supervisor, and the training instructor. They all agree on specific outcomes from the training, and the performance contract specifies how the training will be put into practice. They are used to collect both Level 3 and Level 4 data.

Performance Monitoring – This is the best way to get Level 4 data. It helps you to check the improvement of the different operational data and performance records of the business.

The biggest challenge you will face as a company in this step is selecting the data collection method or methods that will suit the setting, the particular training program, your time and your budget.

CHAPTER 6
EVALUATION METHODS USED IN EMPLOYEE ASSESSMENT

Assessment Centre and Development Centre (AC/DC)

The Assessment and Development Centre service is the most efficient technique used in the inclusive evaluation of the potential of a recruitment candidate. It is made up of group and individual tests done by the participants. The tasks prepared are developed to suit real life situations that the candidate may have to deal with on a daily basis. By simply observation, it is possible to evaluate the professional experience level of the candidates for the jobs they apply for.

Assessment Centre is a group of methods that are used to evaluate the skills of a person and also determining the training needs of your employees. The main goal of the Assessment Centre (AC) method is to estimate and assess the personality structure, skills, and professional knowledge of an employee or job candidate in terms of a specific job.

On the other hand, the main goal of Development Centre (DC) is professional development and self-improvement of employees. The information gathered during this process is used to guide the self-development of the participants.

Applications of Assessment Centre/ Development Centre

Although this approach was designed originally for selecting the best candidates to employ, it now has various other uses:

- Recruitment and Promotion – The participants, who can either be internal or external, are assessed to determine whether they are suited for specific jobs in a company. This is the most conventional use of this approach.

- Identifying Potential - It is important for the company to identify talent early and optimise it. Employees with high potential require continuous motivation to keep them within the company.

- Recognising the Training and Development Needs of Employees – AC/DCs enable identification of training requirements of individuals, while also giving them a chance to understand the ways they could become better performers.

- Organisational Planning – This approach can be used to determine the areas within the company that have great deficiencies in skills, so that they can be developed through training. The results obtained can also be merged with HR data to give an outlook of how many employees with certain skills will be needed in the future.

- Development – Assessment Centre/Development Centre can be used for team building purposes and development of skills that will be in demand in the near future. The employees can undergo counselling and coaching sessions during the programme.

The Scope of AC/DC

- Evaluating the employee's potential

- Identifying the high performing employees

- Identifying areas that require improvement

Steps Involved in AC/DC

- The precise competencies to be evaluated are agreed upon

- The competencies are defined in terms of behavioural indicators

- The required degree of every competency is agreed upon

- The AC/DC is designed.

- A pilot of the AC/DC is implemented.

- The AC/DC process is fine tuned.

- The final version of the AC/DC is implemented.

- Feedback reports are created.

- Each participant/employee is given their individual feedback and development/training plans are created for each individual.

Structure of AC/DC

The approach is divided into 3 parts:

a) *Psychometric Evaluation*

The psychometric evaluation is made up of general reasoning, motivational values, personality questionnaires, personal enterprise profile, and analytics skills test. It makes it possible to identify an employees' potential, their strengths and possible weaknesses. These evaluations can be used to predict workplace success and also serve as a foundation for career decisions.

b) _360 Degree feedback_

360 Degree Feedback is a process used to provide employees with anonymous, confidential feedback on their competencies, from the people who work with them. About eight to twelve people (managers and peers) fill out online feedback reports about an employee. These anonymous forms include questions that are measured on a rating scale, while also asking the people doing the rating to write comments about the said employee. The given employee is also provided with the same form and asked the same questions about his own competencies.

Companies usually use 360 degree feedback system in two ways:

- *As a development tool that enables employees to know their weaknesses and strengths, thus becoming more effective.*

360 degree feedback is very effective as it gives employees an avenue to provide feedback on a co-worker without fear. The recipients of the feedback also benefit because they are able to gauge their own competencies from the perspective of fellow employees and managers. The feedback will help them adjust their workplace attitudes accordingly and develop skills that will lead to job success.

- *As a performance appraisal tool to determine the performance of employees*

Although this is common in most organisations, it is not always a good idea. The 360 degree feedback process could remove the atmosphere of trust within the workplace especially if it is used to measure an employee's performance.

This is because it is geared to measure competencies and behaviours, not skills and job performance goals. The 360 degree feedback cannot measure basic technical skills, sales quotas, attendance, or the ability of an employee to meet basic job requirements. Such things are better off addressed by the employee and their manager during the annual review. Though it can be incorporated into the company's management process, there should be clear communication on how the feedback results will be used.

c) Business Simulation

This comprises a set of exercises that are intended to simulate the demands of the next role in the career of the employee. It provides an employee with the opportunity to decide if they want to take a certain career path, while also giving the managers the chance to recognise employee potential and development needs. Business simulation generally involves analysis of data, role play, and group exercises.

Role Plays – In AC/DCs, role plays should be developed in a way that reduces the need for 'acting' and focuses on how the employee is able to understand and maintain a viewpoint that he/she is not used to. This set up is quite insightful as it allows managers to see which employees are able to adapt and view things from a broader perspective, as opposed to sticking rigidly to their own perspective.

Group Exercises – These are meant to simulate group situations and are used to evaluate how employees interact and talk to each other when solving a problem. The individuals can be given different objectives that conflict with others (assigned role exercise), or everybody in the group can be given a common problem to solve. The important thing is to get them to work together to solve the problems via consensus.

CHAPTER 7
INTERCONNECTION BETWEEN TRAINING/ DEVELOPMENT AND BUSINESS GOALS

If employee training and development programs influence performance and organisational; objectives, how can the impact be measured? Are the training methods being used effective in terms of solving the company's problems? In order to maximise the investment spent on training employees, company resources should be focused on the major organisational objectives. If not, company resources will be wasted on training and development programs that will have minimal effect on the overall goals.

If the tools used to train and educate the employees are interconnected, you will be able to maximise the synergy effect of the total investment in employee development. What happens in most companies is that there is a lack of connection between the departments that recruits and trains, and those that create and implement the organisational goals. A situation then arises where talent is recruited and trained, and then at the end of it all, it is discovered that there is no room to practice the skills the employees have received. Therefore, it is important for the learning to be aligned to the organisational goals.

In today's knowledge based economy, the demand for training usually outstrips the capacity. It is therefore important for the focus of your company to shift towards the most crucial initiatives i.e. maximise the training and show its value. This will help you to avoid a situation where limited resources are channelled to training programs that have very little impact on the overall goals of the organisation.

In cases where the impact of the training is evaluated during the planning stage, the insight focuses on which areas the budget should be allocated. This shift to a predictive analysis model enables the managers in charge of employee training to:

- Be more responsive to present and future development needs.

- Focus mainly on the initiatives that are crucial to the company

- Increase the efficiency of the training programs by choosing only cost-effective training alternatives.

Aligning Training with Organisational Goals

One major decision that a manager has to make is deciding where the training budgets and resources should be allocated. The budget is categorised as an expense, and therefore has to be used in a prudent manner. What every manager should be considering is the amount of time, money, and resources that the training program is going to cost and the potential gains that will be generated in return.

In order to identify the actual benefits, you should first and foremost establish clear connections between the training programs and the company goals. You should determine why the training is even necessary in the first place. Every program that you approve for training needs to be evaluated in terms of how it is going to address exact deficiencies in performance, and what is required to attain improvement in performance. As a result, the training will not be assessed in terms of skills and knowledge developed, but rather by the impact of those new skills on overall performance. What this means is that the training should resolve specific performance gaps or on-the-job problems.

In the event that you discover that the training and development of the employees does not resolve any performance problems, then you should question the rationale behind the training. Remember, if you cannot measure it, you cannot manage it.

The process of linking the different training programs with the company's goals is addressed using a step-by-step methodology, which is described below.

Step 1 – You should define and prioritise your mission and performance objectives. It is not enough to say that the training will develop the skills and knowledge of the employee. What is more important is the consequent improvement in collective performance required to achieve the company's goals.

Step 2 – You should identify the activities that will lead to achievement of performance goals. After the goals have been clearly spelt out and brought to the fore, you should take the tasks that will help in achieving these goals, and divide them into sub-tasks. Remember, the required performance has to be quantifiable e.g. make $100,000 worth of sales every month.

Step 3 – At this time, you must ask yourself "Who needs to perform tasks that will lead to attainment of the set goals?" You should then assign the tasks to different groups, for example sales, customer service, e.t.c.

Step 4 – You look at the attributes of every task (degree of complexity, degree of importance, rate of performance) and then determine which tasks need training.

Step 5 – Rate the skills, knowledge and attitudes that are needed to perform the tasks that have been identified as requiring training. You should be able to rank each skill or knowledge according to priority.

Step 6 – Identify the current and potential skills and knowledge gaps within the company. You can compare the knowledge and skill that the employees have currently, with the knowledge and skills that employees need to achieve the required levels of performance.

Step 7 – Identify any issues that may arise during implementation of the training programs. You should evaluate the feasibility of the training by looking at availability of money and resources, compatibility with current programs, and any attitudes that may interfere with the training.

Step 8 – Come up with a plan of action by collecting data that will help establish which training programs will have the biggest impact and why. With these links in place, the training programs can be realigned any time the goals of the company change, new regulations adopted or new challenges come up.

At the end of all this, you can be sure that every training decision will always be in line with the set desires or goals of the company.

CHAPTER 8
THE IMPORTANCE OF EMPLOYEE FEEDBACK

By now you should have recognised the fact that employees are the most vital cog in the wheel of any company, playing a key role in its growth or failure. On the other hand, lack of feedback or improper feedback can cause a lot of damage to the whole work environment. You can prevent this from happening by incorporating a mechanism that enables the employees to come to terms with their core weaknesses and strengths, in a manner that is reasonable. It is very important to keep the communication channels open so that your employees feel that their input is valued.

There are numerous challenges associated with the modern work environment. It has a changing nature that requires a company to stay on its toes and constantly improve itself. Such a rapid rate of change requires a workforce that is skilled and knowledgeable. This means that your employees have to be flexible, adaptive and focused on the future.

One of the key responsibilities of every manager within a company is to develop their staff. It is important to recognise that the development of employees is a responsibility that is shared among the company, the management and the employees. The distinctive roles played are outlined below:

The role of the company is to ensure that proper programs and policies are used to facilitate the continuous development and training of employees.

The role of the managers is to work with the employees in order to; evaluate and receive feedback on their interests and knowledge; choose training and development programs that tally with their career goals and job needs; keep them informed about opportunities related to training and development; stay informed of new practices and policies that enhance development of employees; conduct a follow up to determine whether the employees are able to utilise their new skills and knowledge within their regular duties.

The role of the employee is to take the lead in assessing their own skills and seek training and development courses that match their needs. They should also work with the management to discover objectives of the training and development.

Roles a Manager Can Play To Ensure Proper Feedback

Coach: As a coach, you can help employees figure out their strengths and weaknesses, values, and interests. It is important that you maintain open channels of communication and encourage your employees. Coaching can be enhanced by:

- Enabling two-way dialogue

- Setting up meetings for uninterrupted discussions about the employee's career development.

- Helping employees identify their interests, values, and skills.

Advisor: You can provide organisational resources and information to employees. Ways of improving your advisory skills include:

- Giving employees advice on the feasibility of different career options.

- Assisting your employees to come up with realistic career objectives that are compatible with both the company's needs and their own needs.

- Assisting the employees to understand the limitations and opportunities present within the company.

Appraiser: This requires you to evaluate an employee's performance openly and candidly, and link this to potential opportunities. Ways of enhancing your appraisal skills include:

- Giving regular feedback in a manner that promotes development.

- Conducting appraisals of performance i.e. looking at strengths and weaknesses.

- Creating a development plan tailored, for an individual employee, for continuous feedback.

Referral agent: You can help connect employees to resources and contacts that can get them closer to achieving their goals. Such skills can be improved by:

- Using your personal contacts to help develop opportunities for employees.

- Provide exposure and experience opportunities, for example on task forces and committees.

Imagine setting out on a long and important journey without signposts or a map – that is what working without feedback is like. Though you may possess a good sense of direction, it may not be enough to maintain you on the right track. Employees who do not get enough feedback will tend to either self congratulate or self criticise; the reason being that they are dependent on events instead of feedback to evaluate their impact and performance.

It is not easy being self aware without feedback from others. Although self monitoring and self awareness can give an employee a good platform, it is feedback from supervisors and managers that can inform them in ways that promote their self knowledge. Employees no longer need to spend energy and time on explaining their behaviour and supervisors and managers no longer need to waste energy in attempting to predict employee behaviour. That is why it is called *Open Communication!*

CHAPTER 9
PROPER COMPENSATION OF EMPLOYEES

What does "fair compensation" really mean? What are the repercussions when the employees feel that they are not paid as much as they should, and how is it possible for companies to address this thorny issue? These are just some of the questions you will inevitably have to answer when deciding on how much to pay your employees.

I have examined the issue of proper or fair compensation from two perspectives; the employee and the employer perspective.

The Employee's Perspective

I believe that the main issue for most employees comes down to whether they believe the amount of money they are being paid, all things factored in, is unfair compared to what they are being asked to do and compared to other jobs they could get elsewhere.

Consider companies that tell their employees that although the salary is not high, they will benefit from good benefits, stable jobs, and achieve important missions. Though all this could be true, the problem arises if the employees do not believe that other job attributes are commensurate with the low wages. Under such circumstances, the company will probably lose its workers, and with a high rate of turnover, this will definitely cost a lot of money. There is also the danger of the organisation attracting people who consider it their second or third job choice – that is, people who are only coming to work for the company simply because they could not be hired elsewhere.

One of the most important factors that determine dissatisfaction – or satisfaction – with salaries and wages is how the workers feel their pay package compares to others. Without a doubt, if an employee thinks that they are doing the same work as someone else who is paid much more, resentment and disengagement will surely set in.

I know that employers look at it in terms of supply and demand. Wages drop if the supply conditions are good; this is rational. But at the same time, as an employer, you want your employees to be content in their jobs. With this in mind, it is just not a good idea to pay people the absolute minimum wage you can probably get away with. You will have employees who are unmotivated and will soon leave to work elsewhere.

Here is something else to consider: employees come to the conclusion of fairness in compensation by comparing their input ratio – experience levels, credentials, and effort put into their work – to their outcomes, e.g. benefits and salaries. They also compare themselves to others in the company or even themselves when they first began their careers. If they come to the conclusion that this ratio is imbalanced, there will be psychological strain that will need to be resolved. The employee might choose to deal with such feelings of being undervalued in different ways; they may think they are blessed to have a job at all, they may switch focus from the pay to the benefits of the job, they may demand a pay increase, or they may leave the company.

Another aspect that I think most employers do not consider is the issue of labour rates vs. labour costs. The wages that an employee earns per hour is labour rates while labour costs refer to cost of production. If you ask most company managers whether they think a raise in minimum wage will make labour costs increase, they will answer in the affirmative. Yet the truth of the matter is, when it comes to low-wage workers, those who are paid more end up working harder. The increase in wage doesn't automatically mean an increase in labour costs; it could potentially result in improved productivity that offsets the rise in wages.

At the end of the day, although companies that pay for performance tend to focus more on the effects of incentives, there needs to be a balance between incentives and equity when it comes to designing the reward system. If you create a wide dispersion in pay packages within the company, the employees are going to find it hard to believe in the fairness of it all. It is always a good idea to limit the range of dispersion in employee pay. This helps with perceptions of fairness, especially in cases where the work is dependent on one another (teamwork) and it is difficult to measure the performance of individual employees.

The Employer's Perspective

What options are available to employers when their employees believe that they are being underpaid?

Under such circumstances, it is best to clearly explain to them how the reward system works, and create a complaint process to make sure there is fairness in the procedures. Another way in which employers can address employee views about unfairness or fairness of pay scales is to use market wage data. This information can be used to help employees compare themselves to others who work in similar job classes, industry, and labour markets.

A major reason why most employees feel that compensation decisions are arbitrary and unbalanced is because the company doesn't bother to communicate well with them about the issue. There has to be some form of communication system where such issues are laid bare. Of course this will depend on the corporate culture of the company; some are simply managed with an iron grip, and such issues are never talked about openly. If your company is a bit more flexible and adaptive, it could try to make a point of providing employees with a yearly printout that explains clearly the employee benefits and what it costs the company to provide them. Being transparent with your employees could go a long way in ensuring that there is trust between management and staff.

As much as I can advise about how to tackle this thorny issue of employee compensation, each organisation needs to make its own decision on its optimal wage. There are companies out there who have low-pay strategies that are beneficial to them. They do not care much about employees leaving and customer interaction means nothing to them. On the other hand, there are other organisations that benefit a great deal by paying their employees well because it makes a big difference in the output of their staff and quality of their products and services. However, I must state that a large increase in salaries and wages does not always lead to more profits. This is dependent on the industry and the market.

CHAPTER 10
MAXIMISING EMPLOYEE POTENTIAL

In today's business environment, human resource management has been drastically redefined and greater focus has been placed on managing employees effectively, all the way from recruitment, to performance appraisal to employee remuneration. This radical shift in HR begins at the most basic stage: helping employees improve their individual performance and maximise their potential, and by extension, enhancing the performance of the company.

Maximising the potential of employees should be one of the major priorities of any company. You should realise that workers who are idle and disgruntled are simply acting as dead weight for the company. They are not just employees working a shift; they are an investment in the company, and should not go to waste. Improving your entire company's efficiency and productivity will depend on how hard you push employees to achieve their maximum potential (with due consideration, of course). Here are some tips on helping your employees become all that they can be - without them hating you in the process.

1. Recognize Existing Skills and Areas of Potential

By examining your employees, you should be able to evaluate individual potential. You could have a situation where your data entry clerk actually has skills related to technical writing or product design. You obviously cannot do this if you do not know your employees, their interest or their past experiences.

Most of the times, an employee who is unhappy is simply bored with their work, and needs to be challenged. If you have certain employee that does not seem to have other skills outside of their role, you could consider giving them the responsibility of training fresh recruits. You can also choose to have a job-rotation system where employees move to different job positions. This will ensure that every employee understands the roles that others play in the organisation, and can therefore substitute one another if necessary.

It is also important to understand the characters of your workers. Some are natural leaders, others followers, while some are innovators. The phrase "knowledge is power" is definitely applicable here. Once you determine the special gifts or skills of individual employees, you can put those talents to good use for the benefit of everyone. For example, once you know which employees are natural leaders, you can train them and then let them train others in the company. It is also in your best interests to let them know of your plans to promote them – this will keep them competitive and diligent. You should also consider rewarding employees who excel with bonuses, awards, or flexible working hours. By recognising their achievements, you will motivate them further, while also making them feel valued in and integral to the company. Let these employees lead and organise company events on your behalf, as they might one day rise to managerial positions.

2. Provide Constant Feedback and Performance Review

It is important that employee appraisals and feedback are up-to-date. You need to evaluate your employees continuously and thoroughly; not only when it's time to raise salaries and wages. There should be a rating system that is fair, where factors like attitude, punctuality, efficiency and teamwork are considered. At the same time, you should talk to the employees about their individual appraisal results.

As you discuss the results of the appraisal, allow each employee to set his or her objectives for the subsequent appraisal, which will then be gauged. This system helps in keeping the employees aware of their own objectives, and they will be able to know if they are on track or have strayed off course. In case they go off track, simply remind them of their set objectives – if they maintain their course, reward them.

Additionally, you should reward employees who take risks and try to think outside the box. It is okay if they fail; taking risks is a sign of a true leader. There are times when having a company full of yes men and people who play it safe can be a bad thing.

Finally, if there are employees who have failed to perform even after all kinds of encouragement, then it may be time to let them go. Make it clear to them that you are parting ways because of their consistently poor job performance. As difficult a decision as it may be, sometimes it is the only way to maximise your employees' overall performance. Don't forget to inform the rest of the employees about why you had to let the non-performing ones go.

3. <u>Make Sure Employees are Engaged and Energised</u>

Former CEO and one of the most influential business leaders of our time, Jack Welch, believed that the eventual aim of managing is not to get an employee to do what is required or expected of them, but to get them to freely go above and beyond the call of duty – because they want to.

It is important for companies to build a culture where the workers feel energised and engaged to perform their duties maximally. This requires the presence of a strong management system and consistency in terms of providing employees with precise and quality feedback. This is not an easy thing to accomplish. However, there is software that is designed to help in human resource management. For example, there are coaching tools and writing assistants that are able to effectively and significantly enhance the general feedback quality. Such HR software can assist managers to provide:

- Better and more applicable coaching – the software gives the managers precise, useful advice for diverse employee issues.

- Richer and more significant feedback – the writing tolls maintain uniformity between managers, and gives enhanced degree of feedback.

- Accurate and more meaningful reviews – the employees get to comprehend their performance compared to their goals.

4. Make Sure Employees Are Aware Of Your Company's Corporate Goals

Making sure that your employees understand the ways in which their jobs contribute to the company's goals is a key step in unlocking their potential. It is important that employees are in sync with the company's overall business goals and objectives. It is crucial that you communicate what the company demands of them and track the progress of the employees compared to the company objectives.

At the end of the day, you want to have employees who are developing their own potential because such employees will always be fulfilled and willing to give the company 100% performance

CONCLUSION

The benefits of training and development of employees is not something a company should ignore. The cut-throat business environment that exists in today's economy requires every business manager to be proactive and forward-thinking. Take the time to weigh the costs and benefits of investing in your employees training and development. It doesn't have to be a large or expensive training program. All you need to do is evaluate the company's needs and the available resources, and see if the impact of such an investment will be truly worth it.

About Author

PaedDr.Martin Prodaj. Lecturer, coach, speaker, published author. Ha has been working more than 20 yrs. on many HR positions in big companies as Amslico AIG, ING, Slovak Telekom, Telefonica O2, Thyssen Krupp, Eden Red and many others. He has been working with individuals as well. He has many experiences with almost every HR tool, like AC, DC, talent management, design and realization of soft skills trainings (presentation skills, sale skills, managerial skills, running different kind of workshops and seminars). He published book Work Life Balance. He is also blogger, video blogger, author of many info products and video online courses. He published more than 200 videos on his youtube channel martoprody

He is living in Slovakia, Bratislava.

You can find more information on his web page www.martinprodaj.com.

Connect With Me

Web page: www.martinprodaj.com

Twitter: @martinprodaj

Connect with me on LinkedIn: linkedin.com/in/martinprodaj

Facebook: https://www.facebook.com/Martin-Prodaj-CoachingConsulting

Other Books by Martin Prodaj

- <u>Perfect First Impression-3 Important Seconds: How To Make Unforgettable First Impression In Business, Work Or First Date</u>

- <u>How to Improve your Business Communication Skills: Perfect communication strategies for improving your life, business and leadership</u>

Last but not least

I must thank you for deciding to purchase my book. I am sure that you had many other options to choose from, but you decide for me. And for this I am very grateful.

I would like ask you for favor. Could you please take a few moments of your time, to leave your review for this book an Amazon?

Just a couple of words...your simple thoughts about this book will allow me to improve the quality of my other books.

Thank you very much.

I wish you the best of luck in your life and business.

If you have any questions, comments, suggestions, or ideas about this ebook, pleas let me know.

If you find any mistakes or typos PLEASE tell me by sending the error and page you found it on to my email

martin.prodaj@gmail.com

Feel free to email me if you need any help to get things done.

www.ingramcontent.com/pod-product-compliance
Lightning Source LLC
Chambersburg PA
CBHW071002180526
45168CB00003B/1257